TERRIFIC TEAMS

# Meet the PHILADELPHIA EAGLES

PERCY LEED

Lerner Publications ◆ Minneapolis

Stats in this book are accurate through the 2025 Super Bowl.



Lerner Publications Company
An imprint of Lerner Publishing Group, Inc.
241 First Avenue North
Minneapolis, MN 55401 USA

For reading levels and more information, look up this title at www.lernerbooks.com.

Main body text set in ITC Avant Garde Gothic Std.
Typeface provided by Adobe Systems.

**Designer:** Mary Ross **Photo Editor:** Elena Mai
**Lerner team:** Sue Marquis

**Library of Congress Cataloging-in-Publication Data**

Names: Leed, Percy, 1968– author.
Title: Meet the Philadelphia Eagles / Percy Leed.
Description: Minneapolis : Lerner Publications, 2026. | Series: Terrific teams (lerner sports rookie) | Includes bibliographical references and index. | Audience: Ages 5–8 | Audience: Grades K–1 | Summary: "The Philadelphia Eagles are known for their superstar players, big wins, and passionate fans. Learn about the history of one of the NFL's oldest teams and meet the players trying to win another Super Bowl"—Provided by publisher.
Identifiers: LCCN 2024060387 (print) | LCCN 2024060388 (ebook) | ISBN 9798765668467 (library binding) | ISBN 9798765683699 (paperback) | ISBN 9798765681893 (epub)
Subjects: LCSH: Philadelphia Eagles (Football team)—Juvenile literature. | Philadelphia Eagles (Football team)—History—Juvenile literature.
Classification: LCC GV956.P44 L443 2026 (print) | LCC GV956.P44 (ebook) | DDC 796.332/640974811—dc23/eng/20250131

LC record available at https://lccn.loc.gov/2024060387
LC ebook record available at https://lccn.loc.gov/2024060388

Manufactured in the United States of America
1-1011741-53814-3/19/2025

Photo Acknowledgments
AP Photo/Matt Slocum, p. 5; AP Photo/Aaron M. Sprecher, pp. 7, 16; Brian Bahr/Getty Images, p. 9; AP Photo/Chris O'Meara, p. 10; George Gojkovich/Getty Images, p. 13; AP Photo/Kirby Lee, p. 14; AP Photo/Matt Slocum, p. 19; AP Photo/Chris Szagola, p. 21; AP Photo/Abbie Parr, p. 22; AP Photo/Patrick Semansky, p. 23. Design elements: Kwangmoozaa/Getty Images; Andrii Shelenkov/Getty Images; AnthiaCumming/Getty Images
Cover: Margaret Bowles via AP.

# Table of Contents

# Fly Eagles, Fly!

Jalen Hurts handed the football to Saquon Barkley. Barkley ran for a touchdown!

The Philadelphia Eagles joined the NFL in 1933.

The Eagles play home games in Philadelphia, Pennsylvania.

Eagles fans love to
cheer for their team!

# Big Moments

The Eagles were NFL champions in 1948, 1949, and 1960.

The first Super Bowl was in 1967. The Eagles played in the Super Bowl in 1981 and 2005. They lost both games.

The Eagles finally won the Super Bowl in 2018. They beat the New England Patriots.

The Eagles lost the 2023 Super Bowl to the Kansas City Chiefs. Then the Eagles beat the Chiefs in the 2025 Super Bowl!

## Best Players

Running back Steve Van Buren was the first Eagles star. He helped the team become champions in 1948 and 1949.

Reggie White was great at sacking quarterbacks. His 198 total sacks rank second in NFL history.

Quarterback Donovan McNabb could run and throw. He led the Eagles to eight winning seasons.

Running back LeSean McCoy was fast and strong. He is the team's all-time leader in rushing yards.

Jalen Hurts led the Eagles to the 2023 and 2025 Super Bowls. He is a great NFL quarterback.

Saquon Barkley is one the NFL's strongest running backs. He runs with speed and power.

★ CHAPTER 4 ★

# Let's Go, Eagles!

The Eagles are one of the NFL's oldest teams. Only six teams are older.

The Eagles have eagle wings on their helmets.

The team colors are midnight green and silver.

The team is full of star players.

Fans hope they can win another Super Bowl soon!

# PHILADELPHIA EAGLES TEAM LEADERS

| | |
|---|---|
| **Passing touchdowns:** | Donovan McNabb, 216 |
| **Passing yards:** | Donovan McNabb, 32,873 |
| **Rushing yards:** | LeSean McCoy, 6,792 |
| **Rushing touchdowns:** | Steve Van Buren, 69 |
| **Points scored:** | David Akers, 1,323 |

## Glossary

**NFL:** National Football League

**sack:** when a quarterback is tackled for a loss of yards

**Super Bowl:** the NFL's championship game

## Learn More


Downs, Kieran. *Football*. Bellwether Media, 2024.

Huddleston, Emma. *Get Ready for a Football Game*. Bearport, 2024.

Leed, Percy. *Football's Super Bowl*. Lerner Publications, 2025.


## Index